For the Love Of

For the Love of Grace

Copyright © 2017 Sophia Latriece

www.sophialatriece.com

Preface

I sit back and take a deep breath before I start to type. The question of 'do I really want to do this' is running through my mind. How deep do I want to go? What would be the purpose of publishing such an intimate work? Am I honestly ready to let people this deep into my life, my thoughts, my personal space? Then I ask myself the serious and honest question of why not? Is it because I am afraid of being judged? Maybe. Is it because people will finally get to know the real me and how I think? Could be. Is it because I'll be opening a can of worms that I'm not sure if I'm ready to deal with at this time in my life? That's a possibility as well. The truth of the matter is that I may never be one hundred percent ready to share my world with the world, so, why not just do it? I mean, what do I really have to lose? And if I only gain the fact of knowing that I was finally able to tell MY story, My way, in My words, well, that's all the motivation that I need.

Many times, we get caught up in the hype of having to put on a mask for the world. To seem perfect while suffering through hell on the inside. We can't show emotion because we will be thought to be weak. We can't show strength, because we will be thought of as being too hard. To be completely honest, I'm quite tired of faking it. Allowing people to view me one way when I'm the total opposite. Letting people think what they want because I don't feel like correcting them or simply because it's none of their business either way. One thing that comes to mind, though, is not to give people ammunition to use against me. If I keep quiet for too long, then I'll become just as cruel and heartless as the naysayers that are against me. At least that's how I see it.

So, here's a glimpse into my life as I've seen it and lived it for the past thirty-six years. A lot of good, mixed with some really bad and a dash of ugly. But for the Love of Grace, I'm still standing; still here to tell my story the way I want it told.

Sophia Latriece
www.SophiaLatriece.com

Introduction

Imagine going through life desiring something. Not sure of what it is or how to obtain it, but, somehow, knowing that you deserve it. Not knowing what it is. Just that something inside of you longs for it. Can you imagine that? Wanting something so bad and not even knowing what it is. It's rather funny, in a weird kind of way. You don't know what it is or how to get it, just that you want it, better yet, you deserve it.

There was a time in my life when I thought I had it all figured out. What I wanted to be, the type of man I wanted to marry, where I wanted to live. Even down to the things that I was for sure I would and wouldn't do. I realize that life has a way of making you change your perspective on things when you least expect it. I've always prided myself on being wise beyond my years. I've always been mature for my age; always seemed to know things without quite knowing how I knew them. I just figured I had some type of insight on things that others didn't. Or that I had seen or heard it before and just couldn't remember where I had seen or heard it.

The one thing that has always been intriguing to me, yet, in some ways remains a mystery is, love. Such a simple word with so many complexities. I had always dreamed of meeting someone and falling madly in love with them and living happily ever after. I laugh at myself as I'm typing. Not because it can't happen; just because for a kid who had absolutely no idea of what love was at the time, I had such high hopes of having it and even giving it. The irony of the situation is that I didn't have the best example of what love really was growing up. My home, as with many others that I knew, was plagued with domestic violence and drug abuse. Now, don't get me wrong, I knew that my parents loved me, it's just that I didn't have a real display of what love was supposed to be like between a man and a woman. Husband and wife if you will. Most of what I knew about love was from what I had seen on television and heard on the radio. All I knew, was that I wanted what they were singing about.

As life went on and reality started to set in (far from the fairytale that I had created), I found myself in a whirlwind which unbeknownst to me, would last most my life and take me to places that I never dreamed I'd be. What's funny to me is that during this process I never thought that I'd lose faith in the one thing that I didn't quite understand but desired so badly. The one thing that kept me alive for so long even when I didn't know I had it. That one thing was LOVE!

1

Sophia a.k.a Peaches. I grew up in the city of Prichard. To this day, I love every minute of it. The good, the bad and the ugly, because, it has made me who I am today. My family was close both in age and physical location, all living within just a few blocks of each other. Every child had a companion. What I mean by that is we all either had a sibling or cousin who was the exact same age or slightly older, so, we always had a friend in that sense. We all stuck together no matter what. We grew up with the saying that if one fights, all fight and we lived by it to the fullest.

I love my city. It's where I learned how to survive; how to hustle. Although the atmosphere at times may not have been the best for a child, I wouldn't have wanted it any other way. My mom was from Prichard and My dad was from Josephine Allen Projects (better known as Happy Hill). I went from one danger zone to the next. Yet again, there is nothing that I would change about it. As a kid seeing all the things that I did made life exciting for me, to say the least. I know it may seem crazy to say, but, I loved every minute of it. You never knew when something would jump off, but you can rest assured that once it did, it was on. From witnessing drive-byes, to drug busts, crooked cops; you name it. It was a sight to see and for some reason, it seemed that my cousins and I always had a front row seat.

I remember one incident in particular. It was a hot summer day. We were all sitting on the front porch minding our own business when all of a sudden, we heard tires screeching. Then around the corner came one car on two wheels shooting at the car in front of it. We couldn't get in the house fast enough. We were all down on the floor in the living room of my grandmother's two-story home. One of my cousins decided she wanted to see what was going on. She got up and went to the window to look out of the curtains. Before she could get a good look, I heard my grandad yelling to her, "Gul, get your ass out of that window before you get your face shot off". He was so scared for her. All I could do was laugh because I pictured her with no face. Some of you may be reading this and thinking that I must be some kind of crazy to say that I enjoyed my childhood with all that was going on. My response would be that you would have had to be there to get it. What's funny is that people will watch movies like this all the time and have no problem with it, but, for someone to say that this was their real life, is a bit more than they're willing to handle.

There were also times, again, sitting on my grandmother's porch where we saw high speed chases with the police or 'Task Force' which was the narcotics unit at our local police department. We witnessed many times how dirty cops would seize money and drugs from people and put it right in their pockets. And, there were times when we witnessed high speed chases that included our very own family members. Those were the most interesting, and for some reason they always seemed to happen around the holidays.

I mean, I grew up during the New Jack City era, when crack had just hit the scene, and everybody seemingly lost their complete mind. You were either smoking it or selling it, there was no in between. And if it just so happened that you weren't doing either, you had someone very close to you who was. Everybody either wanted to be the 'Nino Brown' of the hood or connected to him. It's just the way it was. Fancy cars, lots of money, jewelry, designer clothes; if we could think of it we had it.

I remember having the boosters come to our house one summer with stuff that hadn't hit the stores yet. This was the year the Starter Jackets came out. We all had one. I remember I had Bull's and Florida Marlins (I didn't know the Marlins, but, I liked their team colors). Chile, we were lit, or so we thought. We had no idea of the weight that type of lifestyle carried, but we would soon find out. Seeing family members and close friends hauled off in police cars for simply trying to make a better life for us was a very unpleasant sight. They were working with the hand that they were dealt and at the time, the drug business seemed like the way to go.

My life wasn't filled with just drugs and violence. Like I said, my family was close. There was always something to do, and if there wasn't, we'd find something to do. Like the time we had our clubhouse wars. The boys built a clubhouse in my grandmother's backyard and wouldn't let the girls in. So, we built our own clubhouse. I'd like to think that ours was better in terms of structure and design. The only thing they had on us was that they built a makeshift stove in theirs, so, they could cook. Eventually, God laid it on their hearts to let us in (I honestly don't remember why they decided to let us in, lol; we probably paid them or something) and we indulged in their vittles. The union would be short lived, however, because their club house burned down not long after. Their building must not have been up to code. If you're wondering, no, we didn't invite them to ours.

We also enjoyed the occasional water fight which would spread throughout the neighborhood. We would climb on top of my grandmother's two-story house and jump off (don't judge us). We'd steal one of our parent's cars and go joy riding (who hasn't done that). The one thing that I probably would change is that one time when my cousin almost killed he and I on the go-cart. That was scary. I saw my life flash before my eyes. All I remember is him trying to avoid hitting the humongous oak tree in the front yard and us ending up on top of our heads. Somehow his finger got stuck in the steering wheel, but, we survived. I don't think I've been on a go-cart since.

When I think about it, my childhood was pretty awesome, except for that time I thought I was headed to see the King; Jesus that is. I remember lying on the living room sofa watching television at our home on Palmetto Ave. I heard my mother calling for me. I went to get up and couldn't move. She called again, and I tried my best to move but my tiny little legs wouldn't budge. I was more afraid of what she would do if I didn't come to see what she wanted than the fact that my legs didn't do what I was telling them to do. She called one last time and with everything in me I cried out, "Moma, I can't move my legs". They were literally paralyzed. Just like that. Without warning. I started to feel weak. I tried to turn on my side and by this time nothing would do what I told it to. To feel my body completely shutting down scared the bajesus out of me. My mom came in the living room and asked what I meant by I couldn't move. I told her I just couldn't. She told my dad to pick me up and they rushed me to the hospital. I was so scared. I remember the tears falling down my face because I didn't know what was going on. Laying on the Gurnee with all sorts of tubes in me going every which way. Nurses pulling here and poking there. Everyone speaking in a language that I couldn't understand (the medical terminology that is). There was so much going on that I blacked out. Though, now that I think about it, they may have put me out with all of those tubes they had in me. I smile as I write this because I realize just how good God has been to me. I stayed in the hospital for about three days. My dad carried me in and I ran (literally skipped) out. (Won't He do it)?

I never did find out exactly what was wrong with me. The only side effect that I had was aches in my knees from time to time, but, I still have my life and that's what's important.

2

One thing that my mom made sure of was that she kept us in church. We were very active and very involved. I was a member of the youth usher board and the youth choir. Which in my opinion, was the best youth choir in all the land. Primarily because we had the best musician and choir director there ever was. Philadelphia Baptist Church. It's where I got my foundation as far as Christianity; where I found out that just because people go to church doesn't make them good people, and that adults can be just as immature as children.

I've always known that I was different as a child. The thing about being different, though, is that I was constantly searching, trying to figure out who I was and where I fit in this world. Many times, I came up short and just created my own rules of what I wanted to do and where I wanted to be. Can't say that it always worked in my favor but hey, it's how I coped. There were times when I would look in the mirror and it would scare me because I didn't recognize the girl looking back. I would literally ask her who she was. I would tell her that I didn't know her, and I wanted to know who she was because she wasn't me. What's worse is that I didn't even know who I was, so I didn't know if she was me or if I was the imitation (pretty creepy huh). It got so confusing at times that I would just avoid looking in the mirror altogether.

On top of everything that I was silently dealing with (because I'd never tell anyone that I talked to myself in the mirror; they'd think I was crazy, right?) I started to tap into something that I never knew was there. I started to see things before they happened. I would know what people were going to say before they said it. In school, whenever the teacher taught something new, I already knew it, but, didn't know how. I dreamed about things that no child should even have thoughts of. It got to the point to where I became afraid of myself. I was even more afraid to tell anyone else because I thought that they would think I was crazy and take me away from my mother. So, I did what any other logical person would do. I kept it to myself and found other ways to suppress whatever it was that was going on inside my head.

I started drinking at the age of ten. Seagram's Gin and Absolute Vodka. How does a ten-year-old get a hold to such hard liquor? Well, when your grandmother's house is the 'neighborhood house' and there's always a party, it's not hard to get what you want without getting caught. Now that I think about it, at the rate I was going I'm surprised that I still have my liver and kidneys. All praise be to God for that. The crazy thing about it is that as much as I drank, I never got drunk. My tolerance was too high I guess. Even the more reason to thank God for me still being alive. My uncle said that I had a Tait worm and that's why liquor didn't bother me. I didn't know any better, so I went with it. What's funny about this entire situation is that when I became of age to legally drink, I didn't want to any more. Go figure.

Emotionally, I was a wreck. I kept a lot in. I cried a lot and most of the time, I didn't even know why. I remember being sad and suppressing my emotions, so no one knew what was going on. There were times when I even acted out just trying to cope with what was going on inside of me. I remember overhearing conversations that my family members had about me. About how mean and hateful I was. How I was 'crazy'. How my mom should do something with me, lock me up even. The sad part about it was that not one time did anyone come to me and ask me what was wrong. Not one time did anyone ever try to offer any real help. And we wouldn't dare think of having me seek professional help, like talking to a counselor or psychiatrist because 'black people' didn't do that. That was a 'white people' thing.

How I wish that someone would have taken the time to ask me what was wrong. That way I could have told them how it was all learned behavior because I'd witnessed my dad beating my mom at night. Or how bad it made me feel when I saw my aunt come home one night with a black eye. Or even how it felt to see another one of my aunts trying to hit her husband with a car starter. I mean violence was all around me and all I could do was soak it all in because I didn't have an outlet. Maybe that's why I became so goofy. I needed something to keep my mind off what I was dealing with internally, so, every chance I got I would find a way to laugh.

I became a master of disguise. Unless God himself spoke to you about what was going on with me, you'd never know. I suppressed so much stuff that it eventually lead to depression, which lead to drinking more and still nothing worked. The one thing that I liked doing and I knew that I was good at was writing. I never thought about writing down my personal thoughts or feelings though. I was afraid that someone would find it and I'd get in trouble. More so I'd be embarrassed because people would finally see the real me and I couldn't let that happen. Hell, I didn't even know who the real me was yet. But such is life. I continued just the way it was, hoping one day something would happen and those feelings that I had would simply go away. But, this situation was the least of my worries.

There was a transition coming that I wasn't quite ready for.

One day my mom came in the house from work and told my sister, brother and I that we were going to Disney World. She packed a few suitcases and one of those large trunk cases (that's old school). It seemed like a lot of luggage for Disney World, but, since we had never been, we didn't know any better. We went to the bus station, which was weird for going to Disney World, but again, we didn't question it because we had never been. We were just excited to be going on a trip outside of Mobile. It was a long bus ride to Disney World. It usually didn't take that long to get to Florida, but, we usually drove our own car. We got off the bus and it was chilly for it to be in the middle of July in the south. As we exited the bus heading into the station I noticed that the sign on the front door read Kalamazoo. This wasn't no damn Disney World. I didn't know where the hell we were but I was already ready to go home. She said that it was just temporary, but when she starting gathering our paperwork to register us for school, I knew that we were going to be there for a while. Pissed was an understatement.

We later found out that my mom moved us there with her best friend because of the problems that she and my dad were having. She needed a new start. I didn't understand then, but as I've grown into my adulthood and have overcome some obstacles, I realize that she needed to find her peace. Sadly, she had to move a thousand miles away from home to find it. She told us that we were going to Disney World because she didn't want him to find out where we were actually going. I tried to understand her. I knew she was tired of him and if she moved us all the way to a zoo, then I knew it had to be bad.

My dad had been both physically and verbally abusive to my mom. I had witnessed it many times. It was so bad one night that I woke up out of my sleep and just sat up and watched. My mom came and got me and put me in her bed; my guess was that she hoped that it would make him stop. I remember lying down and reaching under the pillow. My hand touched a large, cold, metal object and when I looked to see what it was, I saw a butcher knife. I told myself that if he hit her again, I would kill him that night; and I meant it with everything that was in me. I was no more than eight years old and I was plotting to kill my dad. Needless to say, he never hit her again after that night. I guess the big guy above was looking out for him.

It was that night that I vowed to myself that I'd never let anyone 'whoop my ass' (my exact words at eight years old), especially a man. I became bitter and maybe a little mean. I was aggressive, and it showed in my relationships to come. My thing was if a situation got heated, I would get them before they got me. I wasn't taking any chances. Nobody was gonna give me a black eye or bruise my face. Not if I could help it. I was filled with rage and it ripped me apart on the inside.

I was torn more so because these were my parents and I didn't want to choose between the two. Still and yet I eventually sided with my mom because I watched her work herself ragged at times to provide for us, while my dad got to do whatever he wanted to do it seemed. Though I loved him, I resented him the day I walked in on him and his brother cooking crack cocaine in our kitchen, on our brand-new gas stove. I felt sick to my stomach. I saw baking soda on the counter and noticed the microwave and stove both going, and I instantly knew what it was. It was one of the biggest forms of betrayal in my eyes. I put my head down, turned around and walked down the street to my grandmother's house. I didn't really respect my dad or my uncle after that. I never said a word to my mother because I didn't want to hurt her.

My dad did a lot of things that made me question why my mom stayed with him for so long. I remember him leaving his lunch box at home once so my mom and I took it to him. We pulled up to his job and the man sitting at the gate told my mom that he had been laid off two weeks prior. She was pissed. I could see it all over her face. She was fire red. I don't know if she was angrier because he didn't tell her, or the fact that he had been leaving the house every morning like he was going to work, when in actuality, he was sitting on the sidewalk drinking with his friends all day. Either way, she eventually got tired of his shenanigans and that's why she moved us to Michigan. (Thanks dad).

I remember being home sick a lot. This made me even more sad. I didn't want to complain because I knew my mom was already dealing with so much, so, again, I held my feelings in and tried to do the best I could.

I was watching something on T.V. one day and they were talking about different forms of therapy. Writing was one of them. I figured it was worth a try since nothing else had worked. I got a journal and began to write down my thoughts. Nothing major, just how my day was going, what I thought about it, and my plans for the future. I was shocked because for the first time I'd found something that actually worked for me. Until my nightmare came true. Someone found it, read it and confronted me about something that was written in the journal. So much for therapy.

I didn't write for a long time after that. Nothing personal anyway. I only wrote what I had to for school and maybe a poem filled with subliminal messages every now and then. By the time I made it to middle school, I felt my depression getting worse and still, I couldn't tell anyone because I didn't want anyone to think that I was crazy or that something was wrong with me. I was a straight 'A' student, with a real family (which is what I was told because I lived with both parents). My dad would eventually join us in Michigan. I guess my mom figured he deserved another chance. I loved my dad, but, I hated him for all that he put my mom through. The older I got, the more I realized that people can only love to the extent that they know how. I figured that he only put out what was put into him and given that his background, wasn't all that pretty, I couldn't expect him to give that much.

I was practically perfect from what other's thought. There is no way that I could let them down. Even if I did feel like I was dying on the inside. I felt like people needed me, so I tried to give them my all and when it wasn't reciprocated it only made me want to retreat. I became an introvert and appeared to most as this mean individual who was selfish and self-centered. The fact of the matter was that I was simply protecting myself from being hurt and misunderstood. I figured if I didn't let people in, they couldn't judge or hurt me. This logic was so far from the truth. The more I kept to myself, the more I was judged and misunderstood and at the time, there was nothing that I could do about it. I simply stopped caring. My thing was, a person could say what they wanted to say as long as they didn't put their hands on me. If there was one thing other than writing I knew I could do well, it was fight, and I didn't mind doing it. These hands got me in a lot of trouble.

Yeah, I was a fighter, but, there was one fight that we were about to face as a family that we weren't ready to handle. It didn't come with a warning label or instructions and it hit like a ton of bricks. I finally realized why my dad came back.

3

It was my night to clean the kitchen and I remember my mom coming in and standing beside me as I was washing dishes. She said that she had something to tell me. I never looked up while she talked because I didn't think that it would be that serious. I thought maybe she was going to tell me that she had finally decided to move back home to Alabama which would have made my entire life. She began to speak calmly; my guess is that she didn't want to scare me. She told me that the doctor had found a lump in her breast. She said she was going to start taking chemotherapy treatments and then radiation treatments. I was confused because I had learned a little about cancer in school and I remember them saying that most patients had to take

either chemo or radiation. I was
wondered why she was telling me that
she had to take both, but, I wouldn't
dare ask. My heart sank, still, I never
took my eyes off the dishes. I asked
her when she had to start taking
treatments and what all they had to
do. After she told me what I wanted to
know, I told her that everything was
going to be ok and I kept cleaning the
kitchen.

Some may think that I was
being mean, or nonchalant or that I
didn't seem to care much. You have
to remember, I'm a fighter and I don't
show a lot of emotion on the outside.
Given the fact that she was already
dealing with this devastating news,
there was no way that I was going to
make it worse. You should also
remember that I was raised in the
church and I knew that the only

person who could do something about it was God.

When my mom left out of the kitchen, I began to talk to God. Nothing too deep. I told Him that I needed my mom and that He needed to fix whatever was going on with her. I reminded Him of how faithful she was to Him and that there was no way she was going to be taken away from me.

Pretty strong words for a thirteen-year-old, but, I meant every word of it.

So, there I was, barely a teenager, entering high school, while my mom was in the fight of her life. I remember going to the doctor with her to get her chemo treatment. I was listening as the nurse gave her some magazines to look at which had different types of wigs in them. She was telling my mom how she could order them, and they would customize them for her. I don't know why but I told the nurse that she was not going to need those. I was shocked when I said it myself. The nurse and my mom looked at me. The nurse just smiled, lol. But, I meant what I said and as it turned out, she didn't need them. Everything that the doctor told my mom would happen because of the chemo and radiation turned out to be just the opposite. He said that her hair would fall out; her hair grew, he said that her skin would darken; her skin got lighter (which was a bit awkward since she's already so light anyway), he said that she would lose weight; she gained weight. So, you see, that little conversation that I had with God that night did pay off after all.

Still, as bold as I was to talk to God about my mom's situation, I didn't know how to talk to Him about mine. I had built up so much anger inside of me that I could hardly contain it. There was so much that I had seen as a child and was unable to express because of the code that most black families have; "what happens in this house stays in this house". I was about to lose it and didn't even know it.

I believe that God has a way of sending just what you need in the nick of time. The problem is that when he sends these things; sometimes in the form of people, we establish relationships that we think will last a lifetime when it was only meant for a season. That being said, I found myself in a relationship with the person who would later become the father of my first child. He was nice, clean cut, and well dressed. He always had money and he had his own car. He was good at fixing things too. For the first time, I felt what I thought was love. He bought me things, which most times my mom made me return because she said nothing comes for free. That he'd eventually want something in return. She was right.

He helped take my mind off what was going on in my house. We had some good times together. The truth of the matter is that I was just too young to be in a relationship. I had no idea of what I was getting into, but, I would soon find out. I thought I was in love. I thought that it was only right that I 'prove' my love to him by doing what people in love do. I was wrong on so many levels. If only I knew then what I know now. The relationship to say the least was very unhealthy. We were both young and had no idea of what we were doing. I thought that I had finally found what I was looking for in love but I couldn't have been more wrong. Besides, I didn't even know what love was. When the relationship began to go sour, I spent a lot of time crying, depressed and even contemplated suicide. I didn't know what was wrong with me. I felt like I was in love with him and when it wasn't reciprocated, I felt like a failure. I felt dumb and stupid and I just wanted it all to go away.

I never stopped to understand that he was a young man who had a lot of growing up to do. At the same time, I was a young woman with a lot of growing up to do.

The one thing that I always knew I wanted was a family. I didn't want to be the type of girl who just went around sleeping with random guys. I wanted a commitment. As I'm writing, I reflect back on that sixteen-year-old girl. I guess she was pretty mature to think the way that she did in terms of the structure of a family, but she didn't understand the true value of being able to grow up and experience life first. She was more focused on companionship and spending her life with someone else, than she was in getting to know who she was and understanding how to love and be comfortable with herself. This would in turn cause a train wreck that she never saw coming.

January 15, 1997; the day I conceived my first child. It wasn't the first time that we'd had unprotected sex. But for some reason, this time I knew I was pregnant. It was like I felt the sperm when it hit my egg. I hid my pregnancy from my parents for almost five months. I had been going to the doctor the whole time. I would schedule my appointments right after school so my mom wouldn't get suspicious. Being that I rode the bus to and from school it made it easy for me to get by. You see, my bus made a stop right by my doctor's office and on the days that I had to go to the doctor, I'd just get off at that stop. My mom worked evenings so she would be gone by the time I got out of school anyway.

How did she find out, you ask? Well, when you share the same name as your mother and the OBGYN calls to confirm her appointment that she knows she didn't make. Let's just say

I was pissed at the nurse for not verifying which Sophia she was talking to. It's pretty funny now looking back, but at that time, I was scared for my life. What's even crazier was that I still tried to hide it, but, on the day that we (because at this point she needed answers) were supposed to go to the doctor my sister was playing around in the bathroom and morning sickness (which is the devil) took over. I threw up all over the hallway floor. That was all the evidence that she needed. My mom was so hurt, and I was hurt because she was hurt, but, what was done was done and there was nothing that I could do about it. Yes, I was young, but, I wouldn't dare have an abortion. I couldn't imagine how a person could do something like that. I guess that was one of the reasons that I kept it a secret for so long. I was afraid that someone would try to pressure me into having an abortion which I was totally against.

October 6, 1997 rolled around and changed my life forever. The day that I had my first child. I was sixteen years old and a mother. There were other girls my age with children of their own but their mothers were raising them. Their kids called their moms mom and I wasn't having that. I was determined to raise my own child and that's what I did. I figured my mom didn't lay up and get that baby so it shouldn't be her responsibility to raise her. The one thing that my mom told me was that no matter what, I was to finish High School; and I did. We ended up moving back to Alabama my junior year. I was glad to be moving back home with my family and being able

to raise my child in my hometown.
Things were starting to look up.

4

My senior year in high school. I was so excited to be graduating from the 'family' school. C. F. Vigor High School, The School that Spirit Built. I had a job, could provide for my baby, and I was getting good grades in school. Life was good and then.....he came along.

I was sitting in the courtyard on lunch when I noticed this boy kept staring at me. Whenever our eyes would meet he'd quickly turn away. I'll admit, I was a little mean(ish) back then (insert side eye). I remember telling my cousin that if he looked at me one more time I was going to give him something to look at. I hated for people to just stare at me without saying anything. She told me who his kin folks were and told me not to say anything to him because there were a bunch of them and they were crazy. I told her that I was just as crazy and I meant what I said. This went on for several days. He would just stand there and stare at me, but, would never say anything to me. One day I caught him looking so I got up and walked towards him. I could hear his heart beating through his chest as I walked his way (I'm exaggerating, but he did look scared). I got real close to him and then brushed past him back into the building. I laughed at myself as I entered the foyer. Little did I know he was about to make a very bold move.

It was a Monday night. I remember because my grandmother and I were watching *WWF Monday Night Raw.* I had gone upstairs because it was about to go off and I needed to get ready for bed being that it was a school night. On the way to the bathroom I overheard Stone Cold Steve Austin say something, so I sat down on her bed to see what he had to say. Just as I got comfortable the phone rang. I looked at the Caller ID and turned away because there was no way that call could be for me because of the name that appeared on the screen.

"Peaches, telephone", my grandma yelled from downstairs. As I went to pick up the phone the only thing going through my head was, 'I know damn well' (because by that time I had a pretty good idea of who it was; the guy from school). But, then I thought, maybe he's looking for my cousin. He was so scared when I answered the phone. I heard his voice trembling as he began to talk to me.

He had gotten my number from my cousin who lied and told him that I said it was ok for him to call me. When I told him that I had not told her that, his feelings were hurt. I heard the shame in his voice, so I asked what was up since he called. He told me that he thought I was pretty and he wanted to talk to me. He said that he was scared to say something to me in person because I always looked so mean. That was why he always stared and looked away. It was crazy because although I didn't want to talk to him at first, it was so easy to. We had to have been on the phone for hours. I remember because we ended up watching the rest of wrestling, the ten o'clock news and *Mama's Family.* We were watching those shows and talking about them as if we were in the same room. We found out that night that we had a lot in common. We both shared a love for comedy, action movies and asketball. That was the first of many nights that we'd fall asleep on the phone together.

Before that night, I had absolutely no interest in him whatsoever. And now I couldn't wait to see him in person and talk to him on the phone. Turns out he was a really good guy. We became very good friends. We talked about everything. And when I say everything I mean everything. There was nothing that was off limits. Except for one particular subject that we just skipped right on over. We never really talked about dating, we just talked about life. We talked about our goals and what we wanted to accomplish. He never even asked me to date him. It just kind of happened.

We were on the phone one night and I started to fall asleep. I told him that I would talk to him later because I was falling asleep. We said good night and before I could hang up the phone I heard him call my name. "Peaches", he said, "I love you". He paused for a moment and there was dead silence. Then he said, "You don't have to say it back. I didn't say it for you to tell me back. I just wanted you to know that I love you". I was speechless. I honestly didn't know what to say. I liked him as a friend, but, I wasn't sure if I loved him yet. I mean, we did talk every single day for hours at a time, but, that's what friends do, right? It was awkward at first, but, he grew on me.

It was crazy because like I said, we talked about everything. His baby mommas (plural), who he had sex with, who he had just stopped having sex with. It was crazy and scary at the same time because there he was telling me how he felt about me, but rumor had it, he had another baby on the way.

I wasn't hung up on that, though, because it was before my time. He was too honest with me for the most part, so I never suspected anything to be going on behind my back even with all the rumors that I'd heard about him. That is until I saw it with my own eyes. I was hurt and pissed because I trusted him. I felt like I had been stabbed in the back and betrayed by my best friend. What I soon became to learn was that we were each other's greatest strength and worst weakness. That was one of the unhealthiest relationships that any person could have been in, the problem, however, was that we were best friends. We fought **A LOT**. I'm not talking about a little arguing here and there. We fought; fist fought. I mean, we squared up. No matter how many times we fell out, we just couldn't stay away from one another for too long. My guess is because we were exactly alike, and no one understood us better than we understood each other. So, it worked for us. I knew he was a whore, and at the same time, although, it would seem insane to someone else, I understood why he was the way that he was. He was dealing with something that had plagued him his whole life and I was the only person who knew about it. I was only eighteen years old and I had no clue of how to help him in that area, other than to encourage him and tell him that everything was going to be alright. He was my best friend, my boyfriend, my lover. People called me stupid for so long for dealing with him. But, they didn't know him like I did. They didn't know the secrets that he held on the inside, afraid to tell anyone because he didn't want to be treated like an outcast. I knew that feeling all too well so, I dealt with the backlash to help my friend. He couldn't risk that, especially with his reputation and his family name to protect. I understood him, and I understood his struggle. I didn't care what other people thought, I finally had someone who understood me the way that I needed them to and I was not going to give that up just because he had issues.

Now don't get me wrong, our relationship wasn't strawberries and whipped cream. And it was full of infidelity on his part. There were times where he was very deceitful, and disrespectful. Like the time he embarrassed the hell out of me in the projects in front of his baby mama. What was so crazy about our situation was the fact that no matter how much of a jerk he was, he was loyal to me in that you couldn't say anything negative about 'Peaches' (me) around him. His friends wouldn't even speak to me if he wasn't around.

I remember riding through the projects one night with a friend and her cousin. We were pulling up to a stop sign when my friend recognized one of the guys walking down the street. He and a guy started walking towards my car when another guy recognized me. He quickly let them know whose 'ol' lady' I was and that they needed to get away from my car.

"He don't play 'bout that one", is what I remember him saying. They turned and walked the other way as quickly as they had come. We all burst out laughing as I pulled off. I got a phone call early the next morning asking why I had been in the projects the night before (snitches). We dated off an on my Senior year in High School up to a year afterwards. I decided not to go off to college because I didn't want to leave my daughter behind. I took the Fall of 1999 off to work and started school in the Fall of 2000.

I moved in my own apartment at the beginning of September 2000. For weeks, he had been asking me to rent the movie *New Jack City*. He said that it was his favorite movie and that he needed to see it. I should have known something was up because

who says they 'need', to see a movie.
We were both movie lovers but, I
couldn't figure out why he was so
adamant about seeing this movie. I
know between the two of us we'd
seen it at least a thousand times.

He came over to cook for me
one night. T-bone steaks and
smothered potatoes. He called himself
teaching me how to cook. I won't lie,
he knew his way around the kitchen.
While we were eating he asked me
about the movie again that, so, I gave
in and told him that we could get it
and watch it the following day.

Monday September 11, 2000. I
was lying in my bed when I heard my
front door open. He walked in the
bedroom holding a Big Gulp from
Circle K and a bag full of snacks. He
kissed me on the forehead and asked

for the movie. He put the movie in the VCR and sat on the floor beside the bed where I was laying on my side. I rubbed my fingers through his thick, black hair as we watched the movie mostly in silence only chatting here and there about our day and different scenes from the movie.

He finished his snacks, stood up and told me to move over so he could get in the bed. He motioned for me to lay in his chest and I obliged. Then came the scene when Keshia shot a man in the head in broad day light like it was nothing. He was so upset. He could hardly contain himself. "How can you just walk up to somebody and shoot them like that. I don't understand how you can just do somebody like that and don't nobody say nothing. Ain't nobody seen nothing", he ranted. I tried to calm him down and tell him that it was just a movie, but he was not having that. "That's bullshit", he continued, "Shit like that happen every day and niggas get away with it".

I mean he *was* telling the truth. Things like that did happen every day. Especially where we were from. I still couldn't understand why he was so upset though. Not then anyway. He held me tight, kissed me on the forehead and asked, "What would you do if I died tomorrow"?

I was pissed. I couldn't believe that he would play with me like that. Why the hell would he ask me some crap like that?

"Died", I yelled at him, "If you died? I don't know what I would do. I'd

probably lose my mind. I wouldn't be able to handle that. Why would you even say some shit like that? What? You plan on dying tomorrow"?
He said that he was just asking. He reassured me that he was not going anywhere. That was the biggest lie that he ever told me.

I got up the next morning to get ready for school and noticed how peaceful he was sleeping as I was preparing to leave. I wanted to wake him to tell him that I was leaving but he was sleeping so good and he looked so cute. He was even smiling in his sleep. I kissed him on the cheek and left. It was normal for us to keep tabs on one another, but for some reason, he felt the need to let me know his every move that day. He literally called me all day long. I had missed calls from him on my cell phone while I was at school. He left messages to let me know his next location. When he finally caught up with me he ran down his entire day from him getting his radio fixed, to having his alarm installed on his car with the remote start. He said that he would be over as soon as he was done.

I told him that I was going to pick up my daughter from my grandma's house and then I was going home. My daughter and I had fallen asleep once we got home and when she finally woke up she was asking for chili. I remembered buying a can of chili from the store, so I went in the kitchen to warm it for her. While I was in the kitchen I heard the front door open. She peeked around the corner to see who it was and when she saw him she took off running towards him. I watched as he picked her up and rolled around on the floor with her for several minutes. He was so happy. I went back to what I was doing while they horsed around in the living room. As I was stirring the pot I saw him in my peripheral walking into the kitchen. He wrapped his arms around me and began kissing my neck. He laughed at me when he learned that I was cooking chili from a can. He told me that I should be ashamed of myself. He pulled a wad of money from his pocket and told me to go to Wendy's and buy her a bowl of chili. I was also told that while I was out I needed to get us (he and I something to eat as well). He said that he had to go do something for a friend and for me to get him whatever I got for myself because I knew what he liked to eat.

He looked back at me with the biggest smile on his face as he opened the door and he reassured me that he'd be right back. He closed the door behind him and was gone. My daughter stood there strangely staring at the door. When she finally spoke, she told me that he was dead. I was so shocked that she would say that. I didn't take her seriously. All I could think about was that I couldn't wait for him to get back so that I could tell him what she had said. I never got that chance because, she was right. He was killed that night. He was on his way back to me. He tried to make good on his word, but someone took that away from him. They took that away from me. I believe that he knew it though. He had to know it. I think he wanted to tell me the night before, but I got so worked up that all he knew to do was to comfort me. I will always love him for that. It devastated me that one of his biggest fears had become reality and there was nothing I could do about it. I waited for him to come back for years. I had lost the love that I had been searching for my whole life (or so I thought) and I was not sure if I'd ever find that type of love again; the loyalty that we had with one another was gone and I was lost. I had to finally let him go because it prevented me from being able to let anyone else in.

Needless to say, I didn't quite lose my mind when he left. Thanks to a very good friend of mine who I love dearly to this day. He made sure that I didn't fall too deep into a slump. At every opportunity, he was there to make me laugh when all I wanted to do was cry. To make me get up when all I wanted to do was stay in the bed. To keep me awake when all I wanted to do was sleep. Thanks T.C. I am forever grateful for you.

5

I ended up taking some time from school after that. I couldn't quite get my focus together. I felt my life beginning to spiral out of control and on top of everything that was going on I found out that I was pregnant with my second child. Another girl. This definitely got me back into focus because I refused to be another statistic. I did not want to end up working at a fast food restaurant or worse (no offense to fast food workers, that lifestyle just wasn't for me). I wanted to be educated and have options.

I regained my focus and got back in school. Although it was hard at times, I was determined not to give up because now I had two little girls looking up to me and I could not let them down; no matter what.

I wouldn't get back into a serious relationship for a while and when I did it was like the cycle repeating itself. Don't get me wrong, he was nice, but, he had a few flaws that I won't go into details on. It was as if the situation with my first daughter's father was repeating itself. Where he and I should have just remained friends, we took it further and everything fell apart. We had this back and forth thing that we did for so long that it became the norm. It was what we did. I don't think that either of us thought that the other would move on permanently. In hindsight, I believe that we were each other's crutch so to speak.

We had gotten to know one another so well; the real us that is, that it was comfortable being together because we were the only people who knew who we were behind closed doors. I also think that we shared some of the same insecurities which we were scared to unleash to the world for fear of being rejected; not realizing that we were doing each other more harm than help.

There was a period of time that I remember praying to God telling him that I was tired, and I wanted something different. I was tired of failing at relationships. I figured that I was a good person, and a loyal person. I loved hard and I expected the same in return, but, I never got it. Shortly after I prayed this prayer I found myself at an event filled with people from my past. There was one person who was there and for some reason always stayed in the forefront of my mind. Though I hadn't seen him in a while, I always thought about him. I was always concerned about his well-being. It shocked me when he approached me after the event given that it had been over a decade since we had seen each other. I didn't even think that he remembered me. He expressed interest in me which took me by surprise because to me, I wasn't his type. Whatever that meant. Plus, we never really talked much in the past. I politely turned him down. I almost felt like I was being punked to tell the truth. I couldn't believe that he would actually be interested in me of all people (my low self-esteem period). There was also the fact that I knew things about him and honestly I didn't know how or why I knew them. Whatever the cause, I decided to keep my distance; not knowing that this bridge would come around again for me to cross, but this time for my good.

I was at a point in my life where I felt like I was at a standstill, spiritually. I didn't feel like I was growing, and I knew that there was more to life than what I had been exposed to in terms of ministry and spirituality. After a conversation with a friend I decided to venture out to different ministries just to see if I could find out exactly where I fit in. I ended up visiting one church and from the moment that I walked in, I felt like I was supposed to be there. It was there that I would meet my now ex-husband. I was apprehensive about getting into a relationship because I had just gotten out of a very toxic one to say the least. Yet, I knew that it was time to move on. I felt like I deserved better and even though change was scary, I knew that it was necessary.

We began dating in the Fall of 2005. He was nice and different from guys that I usually dated. We got along well for the most part. We had fun together which was something that I hadn't done in a while. After dating for a while, I found out that I was pregnant (not again). I had mixed feelings about being pregnant. For one, I was not married and two, I wasn't sure how I felt about the father to be.

Due to some unforeseen circumstances, he ended up moving in with me. Which as I look back on it now was completely wrong on so many levels. I got so comfortable with him being there and being able to help me with my kids that I settled on the fact that it was the life that I wanted. However, I did not want to 'shack', (a subject that I am far more educated in now) so I let him know that he would have to move out until we knew exactly how serious we were going to be. He proposed to me in late December 2005. Again, I had mixed feelings because I was not sure that I loved him. I wanted to love him if nothing more than the fact that I was carrying his child. I accepted the proposal based on me not wanting to be someone's baby mother any more. I wanted to be a wife. I did not want to bring another child in the world without being married. I was sold on the fact that this was it for me. This was finally my chance to be happy. To have the love that I had longed for all my life.

6

We were married on my
birthday, January 15, 2006. I wish that
I could say that this was the happiest
day of my life, but, I'd be lying if I
did. None of his family showed up,
which made me feel like they didn't
approve of the union from the jump.
Not saying that I needed it, just the
fact that in my opinion, they were
blatantly saying that they didn't
accept me. I recall a conversation that
he and I had prior to our vows where
he told me that his mom had said
because she was so close to one of his
daughter's mother's she didn't know
how she felt about him being with me
because she was not sure if she was
ready to move on. I didn't exactly
know what she meant by it and I
never asked her. I told him that she
didn't have to worry about moving on

because I was not marrying her I was marrying him, and she was at liberty to carry on whatever kind of relationship she wanted to with whomever she wanted to. I didn't dwell on that too much; I was too busy dealing with the fact that I was finally someone's wife. Little did I know, it would be a long road ahead. I barely knew how to be me let alone someone's wife.

I know that I'm not always the easiest person to approach so I can't blame his family for not reaching out to me at first. If nothing else I wanted to make sure that I had a decent relationship with my mother-in-law, primarily because he had such a good relationship with my mom at the time. I remember reaching out to her once because my husband hadn't been able to see his daughter as he and the child's mother were not seeing eye to eye. I explained to her what was going on and asked if she could have the child come to her house so that he could come over to see her. She went on to tell me how the child's mother was like a daughter to her and that she did not get in her children's business, so she wanted to stay out of it. As she was talking, I thought to myself that this is the same lady who called my house enraged about a lie that this same child's mother had told her about me. How she defended the child's mother without getting facts. I felt that as long as it was some mess she was all for it, but because I was actually trying to do something positive all of a sudden, she didn't want to get involved. From that moment on I lost all respect for her and chose to keep my distance. His mom died a month after our son's first birthday. What's ironic about the situation is that I called her out of the blue one day as she had crossed my mind. I don't know I guess I just felt like I needed to call her. I'm glad that I did because in so many words she expressed that she needed it too. We talked for a while and she expressed to me how sorry she was for the way that she had treated me, and she explained to me why. I guess you never know what a person is really going through, but, I'm glad that I made that phone call.

Time went on and my husband and I seemed to be progressing. We found out that I was pregnant with our second child together in November 2007. It was a girl. She was definitely unexpected because we were practically homeless, and our relationship wasn't on the best terms when she was conceived. Hell, to be quite honest, I don't even remember having sex during the time that she was conceived. I just remember being really sick one day and thinking that I had the flu. When I went to the doctor, however, they told a different story. Given the unexpected news and our complicated living situation, we still did our best to make it work.

Things started looking up for us and we were able to purchase a house in January 2009. We were so excited that we were finally realizing the 'American Dream' of homeownership. Our relationship was much better, not perfect but better and we were working in ministry together which was awesome given the history of physical, verbal and spiritual abuse that plagued our relationship.

It was Spring Break 2010. We were on vacation and I wasn't feeling my best. I had just gotten a promotion at work which caused me to have to work longer hours, so I figured that I just needed a break. I slept through most of our vacation. Although I was sleeping I wasn't resting. Even after the vacation I was still feeling drained. I even fell asleep in my car one day while on my lunch break. About a month passed and I noticed that I had missed my cycle. I took a pregnancy test and sure enough it came back positive. I was pregnant with our third child. This is not the news I was expecting, but, I was excited as I always am whenever I am blessed with child. I knew that this would be a huge challenge for us financially as well as mentally because we already had two toddlers in the house. I prepared myself to give him the news when he got home from work. I can't tell you how ill prepared I was for what came next.

The look on his face was that of disgust. His head dropped as I told him the news. He shook his head and my heart dropped. He told me that he didn't feel like this was the right time for us to be bringing another child in the world. He never actually came out and said the word, but I knew what he was leaning towards and I was devastated. I figured we'd table it for the night and talk about it later. Two weeks went by and he asked if I had made up my mind on what I wanted to do. This time he actually said the word. I could not believe that this was coming out of my husband's mouth. The minister, the priest of my house, the person who was supposed to be my protection. I was devastated.

It was not like he was just some random guy that I was having sex with, or a fly by night boyfriend; he was my husband. After that last conversation, I started to feel like I had felt a few times before in the past. I felt like I had made a mistake. I didn't see us lasting too much longer after that. Eventually, I swayed his way. I considered being a single mother, raising five children on my own and trying to make ends meet. I was fearful. Although I was working in ministry, it never occurred to me to operate in the faith of knowing that God would provide for me no matter what.

I told my boss that I was having some complications and needed to take a few days off to have outpatient surgery. I didn't completely lie. It was a form of surgery, just not due to any type of complication. It as a selfish act that I regret to this very day. I walked in the clinic that day feeling like I had been hit by a ton of bricks. It was finally my turn to go back and as much as I wanted to turn around, fear wouldn't let me. The room was cold and frightening. There was no sense of life there. I could see images moving but they had no real figure to them. Everything seemed to be moving in slow motion.

I laid there on that cold table and watched them suck my baby up in a vacuum like he was a piece of trash on the ground. The room became quiet. I felt the life literally being ripped from me and I couldn't do anything to save it. I felt like I had died. Right there on that freezing, lonely table in a room full of blurry people who were simply doing their job. I heard him calling for me and there was nothing that I could do to help him. I was empty. I had always felt a certain type of way towards people who had done this and now I was one of those people. I hated myself. I felt like I was the scum of the earth. This was possibly the worst day of my life.

My husband picked me up after the procedure and from that moment on I despised him. He asked if I was ok and I told him yes because I didn't want to talk about it.

The next day I was walking to our bathroom to take my antibiotics and he just so happened to be walking down the hall as I was headed back into the bedroom. He had the nerve to ask me of all things when I was going back to work. I was so hurt. I couldn't answer right away. I couldn't understand how a person could be so disconnected. I knew that I had scheduled the procedure around my normal off day so that I wouldn't miss too much time. I told him that I was going to work the following day. Although I had the day off, I would much rather go into work than to have to look in his face another day. I hated him. I wanted to leave so bad, but I knew that my decision not only affected me, but it would also affect my children, so, I stayed.

In the midst of dealing with this, my family learned that my brother was terminally ill. He had been battling with Neurofibromatosis for years. It's a disease that attacks the brain and causes tumors to grow which eventually become inoperable and the patient dies. This was the case with my brother. He had been fighting this disease for so long and was just too tired to keep fighting. He was thirty-four when he died. It was like a shock wave had gone through my family. My brother, sister and I were very close. He'd be the one responsible for taking care of us when my mom had to work late nights. I remember one Halloween my mom had to work, and we couldn't go out trick or treating. My brother went to the corner store and bought a bunch of 7up candy and hid them around the house. He turned the lights off and we had to find the candy in the dark. It was one of the best Holloween's that we'd ever had. So many memories, so much life gone just like that. So now, not only had I killed my child, I had lost my brother and my mind was slowly going with it.

Just about every night for the next few years, I would be awakened by the cries of a baby or what I thought was my baby. The one that I so selfishly aborted. I knew he was a boy. I even had visions of what he looked like. I saw him looking at me with the most beautiful golden-brown eyes. His hair was sandy red like my brother's. He smiled at me as to comfort me and let me know that he was ok. As much as I didn't want to, I had to forgive myself because I knew that God had already forgiven me for what I had done. It wouldn't be easy at all but eventually (six years later) I forgave myself and started the healing process. I don't think my husband at the time understood the magnitude of what he asked me to do. I absolutely hated him for that. But, because of my faith, I had to try to forgive him as well, if for nothing more than to keep the family together, no matter how dysfunctional it was. I had to also realize that he wasn't all to blame. It was my body and ultimately my decision of what I chose to do with it. I was a coward and I had to accept responsibility for that.

Our marriage was always shaky after that. We tried counseling among other things to try to help but nothing was permanent. Our children started to notice the tension between us and were starting to act out. Our sex life was horrible. Primarily because even though I tried to forgive him, I couldn't forget what happened. I didn't want him to touch me let alone have sex with him. I started to feel like I was sinning against God because I wasn't doing all of my 'wifely' duties, so I tried my best to make it happen, no matter how out of tune with it I was. Sometimes I felt like Miss Celie on *The Color Purple* when Mister would get on top of her and do his business. It got to the point that I had to go to another place in my mind to have sex with him.

We were just going through the motions and no one knew it but us. We always got compliments on how good our family looked and how much people admired our union. They just didn't know it was all a lie and an image that we tried our best to keep up because of our leadership positions at church. Eventually that took a toll as well. I got to the point where I felt I was losing it. I started having uncontrollable headaches. I was blacking out here and there. I went to the doctor and was diagnosed with hypertension. I was thirty-three years old being told that I had high blood pressure. That wasn't good at all. Something had to shake and fast. I decided then that I had to make a move. I just didn't know when or how.

7

There I was, suffering internally with no one to talk to but God because I couldn't let anyone know that the person they looked up to so highly was about to have a nervous breakdown. My depression started to get worse, but I had to keep up a strong front for my children. They were my world and I couldn't let them down no matter what I was going through. I continued to go through the motions of displaying a pleasurable image for my marriage and my home while secretly dying on the inside. I needed an outlet. I needed to do something that would help me deal with my life as it was. I decided to go back to school to finish my degree. I enrolled in the Human Resources Management program at Faulkner University. I liked being back in school. It was a way for me to be away from home having to deal with all the madness there. It also gave me the confidence boost that I needed at the time.

I started to think more and more about love. I even wondered if I had given my husband a fair chance at being able to love him. I resolved on the fact that I loved him, but I was never in love with him. The love that I had for him was more towards the history that we had together and although unstable, the legacy that we were building. I tried to love him more and to show him that I loved him. In the midst of me trying to learn how to love him, I also noticed that I pitied him. I felt sorry for him because it seemed that I had something that he didn't. A mother and supportive family to start. (He later confessed to me that he'd always been jealous of me. That he envied me because of my drive which made him bitter against me. This, he admitted, was why he'd been so malicious towards me at times).

I felt like that once I got my degree I would be able to get a better job which would be great for us in the long run. It was all wishful thinking. It was like the harder I tried to be better, the more he made me feel like I was a nobody. The more I built myself up, the more he tore me down. I didn't feel like I was good enough for him.

He had talked about starting different businesses. So, I did my due diligence as a wife to do the research for him and help him get started. I remember coming home one night and seeing the paperwork that I had gotten him for one of his business ideas sitting on the desk collecting dust. I tried the best that I knew to encourage him, but it didn't seem to work. He told me one time that the thought that I would become successful and leave him. There were also the times that he told me that I was the reason that God wasn't blessing us financially. That I needed to step up in my role as a wife so that God could release our blessings. I don't know what planet he was on but from where I was standing it couldn't get any worse.

We were both off on Wednesdays at the time and this day, he barred me out of the room while he was working on something big he told me. When he finally let me in, I saw that he had put together my very own office space. I was so excited and appreciative. Though my feelings were mixed because I felt like he was trying to make up for the times that he had torn me down. It's was almost like he was saying, I know I haven't always done right by you, but accept this as my apology. I'd like to think that him taking the time to do this was sincere, but, his past actions wouldn't let me accept it as such.

I believe that our lack of intimacy had begun to take a toll on him during that time. It was clear to me that our marriage was over and had been over, but I still stuck in there because I was determined to make everyone a lie who said in the beginning that it was not going to work, and I wanted my children to grow up in a two-parent household.

I got my degree in Human Resource Management and was very proud of my accomplishment. For the first time in a long time my husband seemed to be genuinely proud of me and what I was trying to do for us.

It wasn't long before things would take a turn for the worse. There was a period of time when I started to think about the abortion heavily. I got back down into the slope of depression. I began to question my husband's love for me. I started to think about all the failed relationships of my past. I questioned if I was even loveable. I asked myself if I honestly knew what love was. How could I possibly expect someone to love me if I first wasn't sure if I loved myself? And how could I love someone if I didn't even know what love was? I got in my head a little too much and my life started spiraling out of control.

I started back drinking and going out. I was trying to do anything that I could to get away from my husband without actually getting away. At the time, I didn't want a divorce, I just needed my space. I asked him for a separation and he refused saying that 'believers' didn't do separation. That is the biggest crop of religious bull that I've ever heard. I knew that I needed my space and I had to get it by any means necessary, even if it meant staying out past midnight just to be sure that he would be asleep by the time I came home so that I wouldn't have to deal with him. That logic didn't work too well at all. I remember staying at my mom's house late one night because I just didn't want to go home. By this time things were really out of control and I was tired. I prayed to God on the way home and told Him how I was feeling. I was sincere in my prayer that if this was not the place for me, to make a way of escape as he had done many times in the past. I told Him that this time I would take it and I wouldn't look back.

Two weeks later things came to a head and I left; just like that. I had finally had enough. I figured that my children had had enough as well. It was confirmed by the fact that they were packing faster than me when I said that it was time to go. They literally threw all our belongings in trash bags and carried them to the truck themselves. It's crazy how we try to hide things from our children thinking that we are protecting them. My kids knew all along the hell that I was going through. They were just waiting on me to say the word so that they could get out.

God gave me the peace of mind that I needed to be able to walk away and I did. Not once have I looked back. Still I was missing something. I couldn't put my failed marriage all on my ex-husband. I knew that there were some things in me that I needed to fix if I was ever going to move on and have any kind of successful relationship.

8

I spent several days alone in my new house crying to myself and crying out to God. I knew that there were insecurities that I had to deal with, but I didn't know how. I asked God to show me how to love the way that he loved. I wanted to be able to love myself first and then love others the way that God loved me. For the longest time, I had lived inside of this shell, not wanting to let anyone in and not wanting to give off too much to anyone because I did not want to be hurt again. I realized that I loved hard (at least I thought I did based on my definition at the time).

The truth of the matter was that I was insecure because I had never felt loved in the way that I needed it. I was always looking for it in a relationship with a man because I didn't have it with my dad. He was a good man for the most part, but, he came from a broken home as well, so, I figured he couldn't give me any better than what he was given. I remembered reading in my bible that God was love, so, if He's love and I didn't feel it obviously, there was some type of breakdown in our relationship. I went back to the prayer that I had prayed when I was with my ex-husband at which time I asked God to show me how to love like he loves.

Sometimes you have to be careful what you pray for, lol. I had people coming to me left and right asking about relationships and love and how to deal with different situations. I had to remind God that I was going through a divorce and he had me talking to all of these people about relationships and marriage of all things. AWKWARD!!!!! Please believe, although my marriage didn't work out the way that I wanted it to, I'm not an advocate for divorce. I'm an advocate for peace and I feel that if anyone or anything is taking away from your peace then some major changes need to take place. Up to and including termination. Even dealing with a failed marriage, I am hopeful that I'd be happy again and marry my true love, my best friend. One Day.

People were shocked to learn that I was dealing with such a huge transition and it never showed on the outside. I won't lie and say that it was all easy because it wasn't. There were times when I felt like I was not going to make it. I started having thoughts of suicide but the fact of knowing that someone else would have to raise my children didn't sit well with me at all. I got so low that I began to get angry with God because I felt like he had abandoned me. I kept asking Him for answers. I asked Him to provide for me. I asked Him what I should be doing, and it seemed like He was ignoring me. I felt like he was doing me like others had done me in the past. When He did finally answer me all He told me was that I already had what I needed.

For months, I went through the motions like I had it all figured out just walking around blinded by my circumstances. Etching my way through life, still trying to encourage those around me, while not knowing what my next move was going to be. To add insult to injury, my boss calls us in her office one day and tells us that she has to downsize. At this point, I'm barely making it, I had a little savings but not much and four children who didn't care how I got what they needed, just that they needed, and I was the one who needed to provide it. I needed to make something happen; and fast.

So, remember that one friend that I told y'all about earlier, that I decided to avoid. Well, the bridge was back, and it was time for me to cross. It was crazy how easily we connected. Like we had been keeping in touch for years. He had confided in me about some things that had started to come together for him. We had talked in times before about some things that he was dealing with and couldn't seem to catch a break. To hear this news was refreshing to me. I was happy for him, yet I felt torn because I thought that God was showing him favor and not me. So, I asked God what was it that he was doing that I wasn't doing that he was able to bless him. He took me to Proverbs 18:16 and I instantly shut my mouth. It was in that moment that I sat down and began writing my first book. I had decided that I was not going to let my friend out hustle me. I took out my goal journal and decided that I was going to cross out the goal of me publishing my first book in 2016. That dream became a reality in July 2016 when I released my first book entitled, It's Complicated. I was reluctant to put it out because I'm a writer and I'm passionate about my ish. Honestly, I didn't think people would like it. I was afraid of failing and having people talk bad about me and what I was trying to do. Still and yet; fear and all, I put it out there and got an overwhelming amount of support.

Through my writing, I discovered that I was quite an interesting person with such a vivid imagination. I found out more about myself than I had ever known over the many years that I had 'known' myself. I finally got to know the real me and was able to accept her as she is. Flaws and all. I was on cloud nine. So excited about life. So excited about my future. And then, life happened.

My car was totaled in an accident. My world once again felt like it was just falling apart. I couldn't get around like I wanted to. I had to depend on other people, which I do not like. My children ended up having to switch schools in the middle of the semester. I could not see the silver lining in this cloud at all. I'm laughing as I type because what I thought to be a curse was one of the biggest blessings ever. There were so many lessons that I learned. Specifically, to depend on God with all that I have. My children absolutely loved their new school. The fact that I got to walk them there every morning and walk there in the afternoon to pick them up was very fulfilling to me. I decided to accept what was and press forward no matter what.

I continued to do what I loved and that was write. I found solace in being able to reach people with one of the many gifts that God has so graciously given me. Most importantly, I now understand how God loves me.

For the first time, I felt loved.
Sincere love. Real Love (like Mary J.
Blidge said). The love that I needed. I
fell in love with myself and I fell in
love with my gift. I had allowed fear
to consume me for so long that I
didn't realize it was literally choking
the life out of me and keeping me
from myself. I realized that I had an
awesome gift that needed to be shared
with the world. I decided that I would
not let fear hold me down any longer.
Whatever I put my mind to do, I was
going to do it even if I was petrified. I
said to myself that if it didn't work
the first time that I would just have to
learn from it, tweak whatever was
wrong and go for it again. I fell in
love with myself by using one of the
many gifts that God gave me from the
beginning of time. I can only imagine
the heights that I can reach by using
my God given gifts.

I would have never thought in a million years that what I had been searching for all my life was right here with me the whole time and I didn't have to look any further than the tip of my nose (I just had a flashback of the *Wizard of Oz*. Insert image of Dorothy clicking her heels together). The love that I so greatly needed was on the inside of me the entire time (insert Whitney Houston singing the Greatest Love of All). I just had to tap into it. I was so ready to give it out, that I neglected to receive it for myself. I had to get out of myself, to get in to myself, and find Grace. The Grace that allows me to first love myself and then love my neighbors like I love myself.

I found true love with my creator. The love that He has been trying to show me all my life, but I was so caught up in the things going on around me that I looked right past Him. As of this day I can honestly say with a pure heart that I have found the love within. I realize what love truly is. I understand what 1Corinthians 13 was talking about. I now understand that it was not by my own might but the grace (love) of God that has been keeping me for, so long. Love saved my life. Love taught me how to love. I thank God for *The Love of Grace*.

Letter From The Editor

Some may be wondering why I chose to write such a personal story. Why I chose to 'put my business out there' so to speak? Well, the truth is, just like with anything else that I do, I want to help someone. We go through so much in life and there is no worse feeling than that of being alone. My hope is that someone will learn from my life experiences, especially when it comes to matters of the heart. I didn't know what love was, I just knew that I wanted it. The reason I wanted it was because it was already inside of me. I just had to find it and cultivate it. I was so willing to give it away that I forgot to embrace it for myself. I had to realize that I could not love anyone or expect anyone to love me until I learned to love myself. I could not hold others accountable for what I neglected to give myself. I believe that many of us make this mistake. We want someone and or something to love or to love us and we forget the most important person in the equation which is 'self'.

I'm a firm believer that you teach people how to treat you by the way that you treat yourself. If you have improperly nurtured and cared for yourself, how can you possibly teach someone else how to do it? If you don't love yourself, how can you teach someone else how to love you? I went through a life time of depression and silent illnesses all because I was looking out when I should have been looking in. I had several failed relationships because I did not take the time to grow up; into myself. I was hurt, and I hurt people all because I did not do the work that I needed to do to make my life what it needed to be.

Yes, I could be selfish and say that because I didn't have the best examples that I get a pass, but like I said, that's selfish. We can't hold people accountable for what they don't know. You can only be held accountable for what you know and how you choose to apply it. And to add to it, the people responsible for me as a child may have believed that they were providing the best example that they knew how to at the time. My job at this point is to be able to show my children who will show their children, what true love is and where it can be found. Do I feel like I've perfected this love thing? Absolutely not, but I'm striving daily to become better at it from the inside out.

And to think, this whole thing started off by me asking God to show me how to love through Grace. There were moments when I just wanted to take back what I had asked for because in order for him to teach me to love in such a way, he had to show me the person who I dreaded the most…..me. He had to pick me a part, piece by piece and show me exactly who I was. There were some harsh realities that I had to deal with and it was not at all easy. I had to look in the mirror and finally come to terms with that little girl who was staring back. I had to relive moments of my childhood that I swore I'd never bring up. I had to forgive people who I felt wronged me. Most importantly, I had to forgive myself for the part that I played in my own misery. I realized that I was holding myself back for years because I refused to deal with me. I was afraid of what I was capable of doing if I lived up to my full potential and stopped trying to live up to other people's expectations of me.

I asked God to teach me how to love through Grace, not realizing that the one person I needed to love through Grace first, was myself. I needed to stop being so hard on myself, learn to accept me for who I am and embrace the beauty that lives within me.

It is my prayer that my story, or the portion that I've chosen to tell (smiley face), will help someone find the love they're so desperately seeking so they can live the life that they most desperately deserve.

Just When I Thought It Was Over

So, I went to the doctor because I felt like something was wrong with me. I knew that spotting was normal, but, this time something in me just wasn't sitting well. I sat on the table while the doctor examined me. The moment she put that cold solution on my belly and rubbed her tool across, from left to right, all that was in me felt like it died. I felt as cold as ice. She left out and brought in one of her colleagues whose face dropped as soon as he looked at the screen. He tried his best to hide it. He started typing something on the monitor and then printing each image as he screenshot it.

After a thorough examination of my shivering body, he finally turned to me and said, "I'm sorry, but…….. I simply looked the other way. Tears streaming down my face. I knew what came next and just couldn't bear to hear the words. I held it together as best I could . I couldn't believe what had happened and what made matters worse was that I didn't know why. I was hurt beyond hurt because I was looking forward to sharing this special gift with the world. I felt my world crashing yet again.

You see, after the abortion, I didn't think that I could get pregnant again. I felt like God was going to punish me forever for killing the seed that he'd blessed me with just seven years prior. When I found out that I had conceived again I was overjoyed to say the least, and when I found out that I had lost my 'miracle' I was right back to that place that I thought I'd never visit again.

I was taken back to the table at that abortion clinic, with thoughts flowing through my head of why I must have lost my child. What's crazy is that I have four living children who are in perfect health, but, that one child that I lost hurt me to the core. Not to mention the fact that I had to wait for the baby to pass. Meaning I had to go through labor, to birth a baby that I'd never get to hold, never get to nurture and never get to nurse. I had fallen in love with him, yet I'd never get to meet him. I wanted so badly to go back into my shell of depression and feel sorry for myself. I wanted to ball up and cry for days, months even.

What's funny is that I couldn't. I was too busy thinking of all the women who had been in my shoes and how they must have felt. I wanted to learn how to deal with it so that I could help someone else. I thought about the many women who have never been able to bear children. How selfish of me would it be to wallow in self-pity knowing that I had four beautiful children of whom I didn't plan and there were millions of women who wanted them and couldn't have them on their own? It also made me appreciate the process of life altogether. I realized that all lives are miracles.

So, you see while I was learning to love through Grace, I also learned how to hope. Hope in the fact that with everything that has gone on in the short time that I've been on this earth, I believe that things can only get better from here. I have a hope that Grace will continue to lead and teach me. I have a hope that even if I'm never able to conceive again, that I'd learn to be ok with it because there is great work to do on this earth and many spiritual birthings that need to take place.

Grace provides the ability to overcome the pain, hope provides the strength to live through it. Without death there can be no life. Besides, what's life without having been raised from the dead?

www.ingramcontent.com/pod-product-compliance
Lightning Source LLC
Chambersburg PA
CBHW061743020426
42331CB00006B/1339